Happy Holidays!

Thanksgiving

by Betsy Rathburn

BELLWETHER MEDIA
MINNEAPOLIS, MN

Blastoff! Beginners are developed by literacy experts and educators to meet the needs of early readers. These engaging informational texts support young children as they begin reading about their world. Through simple language and high frequency words paired with crisp, colorful photos, Blastoff! Beginners launch young readers into the universe of independent reading.

Sight Words in This Book

a	day	it	see	time
an	eat	of	some	to
and	for	on	the	what
are	in	people	there	
big	is	say	they	

This edition first published in 2023 by Bellwether Media, Inc.

Library of Congress Cataloging-in-Publication Data

Names: Rathburn, Betsy, author.
Title: Thanksgiving / by Betsy Rathburn.
Description: Minneapolis, MN : Bellwether Media, 2023. | Series: Blastoff! beginners. Happy holidays! | Includes bibliographical references and index. | Audience: Ages 4-7 | Audience: Grades K-1
Identifiers: LCCN 2022009282 (print) | LCCN 2022009283 (ebook) | ISBN 9781644876848 (library binding) | ISBN 9781648348600 (paperback) | ISBN 9781648347306 (ebook)
Subjects: LCSH: Thanksgiving Day--Juvenile literature.
Classification: LCC GT4975 .R37 2023 (print) | LCC GT4975 (ebook) | DDC 394.2649--dc23/eng/20220224
LC record available at https://lccn.loc.gov/2022009282
LC ebook record available at https://lccn.loc.gov/2022009283

Editor: Christina Leaf Designer: Laura Sowers

Printed in the United States of America, North Mankato, MN.

Table of Contents

It Is Thanksgiving!

The family
is together.
Time to eat.
Happy
Thanksgiving!

A Day to Give Thanks

Thanksgiving is in November. It is on the fourth Thursday.

It is an
American holiday.
It is a day
to give thanks!

People see family.
They see friends.

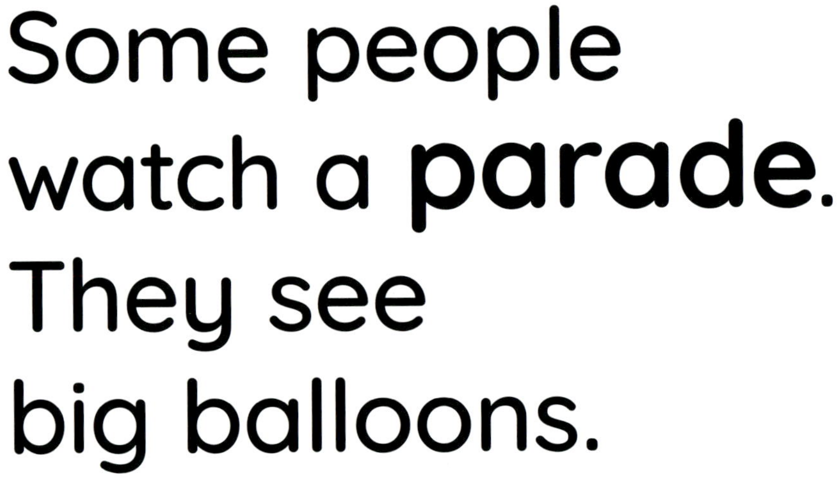

Some people watch a **parade**. They see big balloons.

parade

Some people watch football. They cheer.

football

People say what they are **thankful** for.

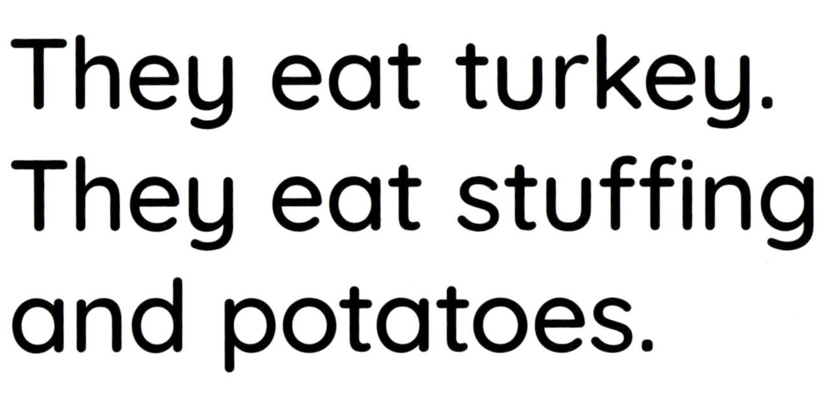

They eat turkey. They eat stuffing and potatoes.

potatoes

They eat pie for **dessert**. There is a lot of food!

Thanksgiving Facts

Celebrating Thanksgiving

Thanksgiving Activities

watch a parade

give thanks

eat turkey

Glossary

dessert

a sweet food eaten after a main meal

parade

a line of people or groups who walk together during events

thankful

happy about something

To Learn More

ON THE WEB

FACTSURFER

Factsurfer.com gives you a safe, fun way to find more information.

1. Go to www.factsurfer.com.
2. Enter "Thanksgiving" into the search box and click 🔍.
3. Select your book cover to see a list of related content.

Index

The images in this book are reproduced through the courtesy of: lhmfoto, front cover; LightField Studios, p. 3; Monkey Business Images Ltd/ Getty, pp. 4-5; skynesher, pp. 6-7; manonallard/ Getty, pp. 8-9; monkeybusinessimages, pp. 10-11; NYC Russ, p. 12; ALEXIUZ, pp. 12-13; Cherdchai charasri, p. 14; Cal Sport Media/ Alamy, pp. 14-15; Jaren Jai Wicklund, p. 16; Marina Andrejchenko, pp. 16-17; Bochkarev Photography, p. 18; Monkey Business Images, pp. 18-19, 22 (give thanks, eat turkey), 23 (thankful); Pixel-Shot, p. 20; LightFieldStudios, pp. 20-21; Brent Hofacker, p. 22; Ron Adar, p. 22 (parade); pilipphoto, p. 23 (dessert); Hoover Tung, p. 23 (parade).